```
I0201404
```

A Marriage To Beat All Odds

Insights from the Marriage of Mary and Joseph

Ray W. Lincoln

A Marriage To Beat All Odds

(Formerly *Willed in Heaven and Made to Work on Earth*)

© 2006 by Ray W. Lincoln
All rights reserved.

No part of this book may be reproduced or transmitted in any form or by any means, electronic or mechanical, including photocopying, recording, or by any information storage and retrieval system, except as may be expressly permitted by the 1976 Copyright Act or in writing from the publisher. Requests for permission can be addressed to Permissions, Apex Publications, 520 Chestnut Oak, Ingram, TX 78025-3284 or emailed to solutions@raywlincoln.com.

ISBN: 978-0-9996349-7-4

2006 Printed in New Zealand
2008 Printed in the United States
2020 Revised

Apex Publications
Ingram, Texas

© 2020 Ray W. Lincoln

Dedication

Many of my days, I have needed the touch of an expert. An expert is someone you trust and someone who has proved his or her wisdom, concern and intelligence in matters in which you judge him or her to be your superior. Feelings of self-worth are not destroyed when you place yourself in that person's care.
In fact, it makes you feel all the more worthy to be judged worthy of that person's expert attention.
In matters of the marriage relationship, the expert needs to display one more quality that is the most important of all — love.
Thank you to my expert partner in the joys and adventures of mutual submission and love, Mary Jo.

"A happy marriage is one where you both feel you get more than you deserve." ~Anonymous

"Love never fails." ~1Corinthians 13:8

© 2020 Ray W. Lincoln

Acknowledgements

Like marriage, a book is built
One act of love on another,
Each deepening a sense of gratitude
Until gratefulness runs deep and strong
In the mysterious depths of the human spirit
To feed and refresh after toil.

I wish to express my thankfulness for the labors of my wife, Mary Jo, for her selfless sacrifices.

© 2020 Ray W. Lincoln

Contents

© 2020 Ray W. Lincoln

A Marriage to Beat All Odds
(Insights from the marriage of Mary and Joseph)

A study of the marriage relationship of Joseph and Mary has not often been attempted simply because it is assumed we know so little about it. On the contrary, I think we know almost all the important things we need to know about their marriage, or any marriage. We'll begin our defense of the above claim with a provocative question that should help us find some answers for their marriage, which beat all the odds in earth's hostile conditions.

© 2020 Ray W. Lincoln

Should Mary and Joseph Have Married?

Did Joseph make the right decision in marrying Mary when she was found to be "mysteriously" pregnant before marriage and Joseph knew the child wasn't his?

History says, "Yes, of course; because the child was the Savior of the world and the greatest person who ever lived on this planet." The question we are asking, however, is whether it was a marriage that you or I would have recommended or discouraged had Joseph come to us for advice?

Discouraged

Wasn't it clear that Mary couldn't be trusted? Is it advisable to enter into a commitment — because that's what marriage is — when your fiancé has become pregnant and you know you haven't even had sex with her? If left to our judgment, the Savior would have been the child of a single mother.

Perhaps it would be good to pause and remind ourselves why human judgments can so easily be wrong. We simply do not know everything. Give me all the facts and I am less likely to be wrong in my opinion. Tell me only some of the details, and my judgment must remain uncertain at best. Joseph simply did not know enough to wisely make this decision, and if we had been his friends, we too would

© 2012 Ray W. Lincoln

be lacking in the one crucial element that could change the advice.

But what of Joseph's personal feelings? Did he handle well the slippery feelings of doubt that must have assailed him from time to time — particularly when stresses over money or family hit — or had he found peace? Were the trouble and the ostracism that he received from a very conservative society for marrying Mary worth it?

I think so. But that's easy for me to say. However, after considering my armchair opinion, I still think Joseph would have made the same decision again had God asked him to. Why? Because Joseph and God had a special relationship going — that much we do know. As you read on you will find out what that special relationship was.

Did the Marriage Have a Good Chance of Being Fulfilling?

One must suppose the marriage was not without its blessings and love, since God was so heavily involved and both Joseph and Mary showed such commitment to each other. Joseph may also have felt the power of God's goodness surrounding him and sustaining him when others looked sideways at him because he had taken a pregnant woman as his wife.

The marriage was virtually an admission of sex before marriage on Joseph's part, and was (in the eyes of that

© 2020 Ray W. Lincoln

society) next to a crime. How did it affect his ability to build his carpentry business, I wonder. Was he scraping hand-to-mouth, or did he get most of his business from the building of a Greek town nearby? This providential happening no doubt did have a positive effect on some of the inhabitants of Nazareth and may have also conditioned Jesus in his early years to Greek influences and thinking.

If Joseph had not taken responsibility for Mary's condition, she would have been charged, tried at the city gate, and stoned! Such was the law in Palestine two millennia ago, although there is evidence that the Nazarenes might not have taken the law to its literal conclusion.

Why do I feel reasonably sure that Joseph was at peace over his marriage? Well, I'm going out on a limb, so to speak, which means I have only indirect evidence for my first reason.

It's an opinion based on an ethical principle that governs all of life. James uses this principle to convince us in his third chapter that bad talk can only come from a bad mind, and good talk can only come from a good mind. "Pure and foul water can't come from the same spring," he argues. This is an ethical principle, operative in a moral universe, and ours is a moral world. The certainty of this moral truth compares to the certainty of the law of gravity.

If good doesn't produce bad, and bad doesn't source good, then can we argue that a relationship with such an obvious claim to being made in heaven would be a certain cause of a peaceful heart? I think so. Therefore, something of such great blessing to the world as the birth and upbringing of no less than the Son of God must have happened in a home that was a blessing in itself. Not least, Jesus' presence would surely have made for a wonderful home.

So, following this indirect reasoning from a moral principle, we conclude that Jesus came from a good home and even rose above its goodness because he was of divine as well as human origin.

Let's remember, they should have gotten married because God prepared and chose this relationship to nurture Jesus. And God makes no mistakes. That's my second reason, and this one is on solid ground!

Finally, since God always rewards goodness and obedience to his will, I also think he must have rewarded Joseph for his obedience in this matter.

Let's sum up our reasoning:

1. A foul spring doesn't produce pure water.
2. God makes no mistakes.

© 2020 Ray W. Lincoln

3. God sees to it that goodness and obedience are rewarded.

Therefore, the home we know so little about was, I feel safe in saying, a home blessed by God and fulfilling to Joseph and Mary. The same principles operating in our homes will produce the same results.

© 2020 Ray W. Lincoln

© 2020 Ray W. Lincoln

God's Will Is the "Building Permit" for a Great Marriage

This is where all marriages should start: in the will of God. In an age of individualism, where it is frowned upon to suggest that one might wisely seek approval for one's decision to marry, I think we need more than ever to encourage people to seek God's will before entering into the marriage vows. Individualism is not a virtue! Rejection of authority smacks of a modern mind freed from the restraints that inhibit individualism and it, too, is a damaging principle. If you don't want to accept the Word of God that makes the authority of God and the Lordship of Christ fundamental maxims of one's relationship with God, accept at least the witness of history that reminds us that where authority is rejected, the cords that hold society in healthy balance are severed and society is in danger of anarchy. Am I a scaremonger? Not if the repeated lessons of history are to be allowed a hearing.

Joseph and Mary's marriage certainly started in the will of God and with recognition of God's authority over their lives. The story emphasizes the part God's will played in their decisions. The angel's messages to both Joseph and Mary are, no doubt, on view in heaven's museum!

We talk of marriages made in heaven. Marriages are, indeed, *willed* in heaven but *made* to work on earth. So,

© 2020 Ray W. Lincoln

start with heaven's will, and aim to make a little heaven on earth out of the marriage relationship God has given you.

What If I Didn't Seek God's Will for My Marriage?

But what if your marriage was formed on your will, not God's will? Perhaps you didn't consult God! Then here is good news: you can apply for an exemption!

Sound odd? Not really, because God is a God of re-creation, of new beginnings, of making great things — even out of nothing. Didn't he make the world out of nothing?

Furthermore, your present marriage relationship is not "nothing." It's made up of two people who have been created in God's image and have unlimited potential.

However, when your spouse is lazing on the couch, it may not look to you like unlimited potential. But believe me, we can all astonish even our spouses when the creative fingers of God are at work in us.

God grants exemptions when we fail to do his will because his grace is sufficient for any and all of us. No paperwork is needed, just a prayer. Thank God for what you have. He accepts us as we are.

Exemptions are God's way of saying, when we have made a mistake in not consulting him, that all is not lost. He has

© 2020 Ray W. Lincoln

a path for us to happiness and peace that leads through the door of forgiveness and grace to a new and better world.

Change Where Change Is Needed

We must believe in both God's abilities and our own. ***"I can do all things through Christ who strengthens me,"*** Paul insists in Philippians 4:13. It's not just God who can do the impossible. It's also God in and with us. Believe it! If you don't, you turn away from a human's greatest hope. Of course, we *can* change with help like this! I have heard this question perhaps more than any other, "Do you think my spouse can *really* change?"

When a relationship sours, both partners doubt each other. Coming to faith in each other again is not only possible, but essential — a gift God is waiting for us to open and enjoy. Rebuilt faith is even better than the initial faith we had in each other, because it is now a tried and tested faith and a faith that tastes of a fresh, divine element: forgiveness. In fact, it is even more than this. It is God's offer to lift us up to a self-realization of what creatures made in his own image can achieve and become. It is a taste of our highest potential.

Nothing is impossible with God. Don't believe the Devil's lie that your relationship has reached a place where it is impossible for it to be renewed, rewarding, and totally fulfilling. I can't believe that when I know that nothing is impossible for God, and all that has to happen to renew

© 2020 Ray W. Lincoln

that relationship is for two nice people to renew their submission to God and each other. I can believe, however, that some people won't submit to God's regenerating power (a fact all of us are guilty of at times). And that's where many breakups occur. This demeaning use of our free will stains us all, and we must accept responsibility for it.

So, I believe, even the most stressed-out relationship can be renewed if we will let it happen and not oppose it.

Many couples have told me, "It's all over, and there's no reason to stay in a relationship that is damaging both parties." Of course, they usually don't remind me that it is damaging because of their poor attitudes and unforgiving, self-centered hearts — something we are all guilty of at times.

© 2020 Ray W. Lincoln

Forgiveness – The Sweetest Gift We Can Give Each Other
?? ??

A good marriage starts in heaven but is made on earth, and the making of it begins with two nice, forgiving people.

This forgiveness we are talking about played a real role in Joseph and Mary's relationship, even though their relationship was made in heaven. Joseph must have told Mary a thousand times that he was sorry for not believing her. It must have hurt her even though she realized the strain it would put on Joseph's credulity. As important as the angel's visit was to him, it was also a reminder that it took an angel's visit to get him to believe his fiancé! The first tool you will find in your bag for relationship repair is "forgiveness." If you are "normal," you will use it many, many times in your marriage. You will come to appreciate its positive power and its sweet aftereffects.

Forgiveness doesn't put down the one who seeks it or is offered it. The word contains the word "give." Forgiveness is the giving of one of life's most precious gifts. The giver is blessed by an act designed by God and, in forgiving, reflects his nature, while the receiver unwraps and treasures a gift especially designed by God to warm and repair relationships. Could there be a better gift to give each other?

© 2020 Ray W. Lincoln

Whenever we have failed, there is a simple path to rebuilding our relationships: forgiveness. God is SO good!

© 2020 Ray W. Lincoln

⁇ ⁇

Was It the Marriage of Mary and Joseph Or of Joseph and Mary?

⁇ ⁇

This is truly a postmodern conundrum! I would say it was the marriage of "Joseph and Mary" if I wanted to reflect the customs of that day. The male was always listed as the one responsible, both legally and socially, in the marriage and was listed first in public notices. However, if I reflect on who was the most famous, it's "Mary and Joseph." This points out one of the possible and frequent areas of friction in marriages: Who's number one? And for that matter, does there have to be a number one?

This, in turn, raises another dispute: how are matters settled in a marriage when two can't agree and there isn't a casting vote or a third vote to create a majority? How do two equal votes that are cast for opposing interests settle an issue? They don't!

Of course, if the votes are not equal — say in the case of the husband having a more important vote — then there isn't a problem in determining issues over which the partners in the marriage are split. The husband rules.

Some husbands actually like this. They feel they have the support of the Bible, because it says, *"...wives submit to your husbands... for the husband is the head of the*

© 2020 Ray W. Lincoln

wife...," and they apply these words *out of their context* to their benefit. One man even left a church where I was senior pastor when I pointed out his error in the way he was using these passages because, as he said, "What is the use of supporting a church that doesn't support what I believe." That reasoning is like trying to find a Bible and a god that agree with you.

In Joseph's day the votes weren't equal. The male did indeed have the deciding or casting vote, and some would indicate "the only vote." Then it should surprise you that the marriage of Mary and Joseph provides an answer to this apparently modern problem of who has the last say when the votes are equal.

Both Mary and Joseph believed the child to be of God's instigation by way of a miracle. Was Mary then the most important, since God had given her the child? Was Joseph to play a second-string role since he had been bypassed, so to speak? Or were they to live by the customs of their day and let the male rule? Let's discover how this unfolded.

© 2020 Ray W. Lincoln

Submission to God Should Give Birth to Submission to Each Other

In the governance of their home, I have the feeling that Mary and Joseph may have been the first couple in the New Testament to make a marriage work God's way. Of course, what I am intimating here is that God's way may be quite different from the legal and social way demanded by their culture — or any culture. Cultural factors are as slippery a standard as are traditional ways of doing things. I am also suggesting that no matter what the demands of the culture, be it oppressive to females or not, God's way can still be followed in the private relationships of a Christian home.

Let me explain what God's plan is for marriage relationships and for the working out of differences. We'll use Mary and Joseph as our surprising examples.

Mary was the first to encounter God in the unique entanglements of this relationship. Before she was married to Joseph, God said to her:

> *"Greetings. You are highly favored, the Lord is with you." Mary was greatly troubled at his words and wondered what kind of greeting this might be. But the angel said to her, "Do not be afraid, Mary,*

© 2020 Ray W. Lincoln

you have found favor with God. You will be with child and give birth to a son, and you are to give him the name Jesus. He will be great and will be called the Son of the Most High. The Lord God will give him the throne of his father David, and he will reign over the house of Jacob forever; his kingdom will never end." "How will this be," Mary asked the angel, "since I am a virgin?" The angel answered, "The Holy Spirit will come upon you and the power of the Most High will overshadow you. So the holy one to be born will be called the Son of God. Even Elizabeth your relative is going to have a child in her old age, and she who was said to be barren is in her sixth month. For nothing is impossible with God." "I am the Lord's servant," Mary answered, "May it be to me as you have said." Then the angel left her. [Luke 1:28-38]

In this exchange, it seems obvious to me that God was taking a very strong hand in directing Mary's life. What is more important, I note that Mary goes along with God's plan, even though she doesn't understand it.

© 2020 Ray W. Lincoln

This submission to the will of God when we don't understand sets the stage in Mary's heart to do things God's way, whatever the outcome. God's way of living always begins with submission to him first, and then the other problems of our lives can be sorted out.

Joseph also had a word from God:

> *This is how the birth of Jesus Christ came about. His mother, Mary, was pledged to be married to Joseph, but before they came together, she was found to be with child through the Holy Spirit. Because Joseph, her husband, was a righteous man and did not want to expose her to public disgrace, he had in mind to divorce her quietly. But after he had considered this, an angel of the Lord appeared to him in a dream and said, "Joseph, son of David, do not be afraid to take Mary home as your wife, because what is conceived in her is from the Holy Spirit. She will give birth to a son, and you are to give him the name Jesus, because he will save his people from their sins." All this took place to fulfill what the Lord had said through the prophet: "The virgin will be with child and will give birth to a son, and they will*

© 2020 Ray W. Lincoln

call him 'Immanuel' which means, 'God with us.'"   When Joseph woke up, he did what the angel of the Lord had commanded him and took Mary home as his wife.   But he had no union with her until she gave birth to a son. And he gave him the name Jesus. [Matthew 1:18-24]

Joseph also appears to want God's way. He submits to God's will and agrees to the marriage, even though this will cost him the disdain and scorn of his friends and countrymen.

Both Mary and Joseph Independently Determined to Submit to God's Will
A good outcome for this marriage is almost certainly signaled by their willing submission to God, don't you think?

So, is submission to God the first step in positive, potentially satisfying relationships. Or is it something more than just a first step? More!

It's more like a *way of living*, not just a first step. God's way in human relationships (our relationship to him included, of course) is to learn to submit. Submission in marriage is best taught and understood, first, in our experience of submitting to God. This is how Mary and Joseph began a new way of living with God and each

© 2020 Ray W. Lincoln

other. In the discipline of our submission to God we refine and tune our submission to each other.

When we submit to God (God being so loving and gracious), we learn that submission is not a negative experience. It is something that brings all kinds of blessings. Rewarding relationships are only possible through this two-way flow of respect and love.

When two people marry, respect and love must be encouraged or love will die. Submission is the atmosphere in which respect and love grow, and a positive uplifting experience is the result.

Beginning your relationship together in marriage by first submitting to God's will creates another unexpected blessing. It not only prepares us for each other, but it's no longer the two of us. There are three of us — me, my partner, and God — who are facing life's unknowns together. Submit to God's will and there are three of you to solve life's problems!

On this unknown journey that both are taking by faith into the future, we can have help. We think we know our partner, but the truth is we only know him or her in part. God is the only one who knows both of us completely. We are individually created according to a plan he has for us. And our unique personalities and temperaments will cause many a fusion or fracture in our relationship if we don't

© 2020 Ray W. Lincoln

recognize we are in need of help. The outcome of your relationship — its path, its hurdles, its rewards — is all a matter of the unknown future. You'll need a guide; and you'll need to submit to that Guide and his leadership. That Guide is no help if we ignore Him.

Best to incorporate that Guide as your enabling partner, taking him into the relationship, don't you think? And what better guide to have than a God who knows the future and holds you in his hand? So, learning to submit to God prepares our spirits for the real tough task that lies ahead — the task of making a marriage work — while it heaps blessings on us, too. Is submission beginning to sound as though it has some benefits?

Mary and Joseph settled the matter of submission to God and then, no doubt, carried this spirit into their marriage. When both partners are submitting to God, an automatic solution emerges to the problem of who is number one.

Submission Is the Key, But Who Submits to Whom
Now, who is it that must submit to the other in a marriage relationship if God's way is to be followed? This is that million-dollar question that bothers so many partners in marriage. Particularly if one has a dominating element in his or her personal makeup, this can become a battle ground for dominance. We know we both must submit to God. But is it the wife or is it the husband who has to do

© 2020 Ray W. Lincoln

the submitting to the other? Another possibility suggests itself: does either have to be number one?

I have a surprise ahead for many of you who have read your Bible or listened to well-meaning preachers quoting Ephesians 5:22. A hint of the surprise is in our story, because it looks like Joseph had to submit to Mary by trusting her.

For Joseph, the task of submitting to being the father of a baby boy who wasn't his son and, in the process, submitting to a wife who asked for his trust when it didn't look reasonable to give it, could have been a big emotional hurdle. Perhaps the crucial conversation went like this:

> "I haven't been with another man, Joseph. I told you what God told me. Doesn't that mean anything to you?" Mary pleads.

> "And you expect me to believe you are pregnant without a man? Come on, Mary. I wasn't born yesterday. My father told me the facts of life!" replies Joseph.

> "Joseph," begs Mary, "I'm not lying to you, I swear I'm not. If you really love me, you will surely believe me."

Mary breaks down in tears and Joseph is left with two alternatives. He either must (1) trust Mary and submit to her pleading, or (2) decide she has to be someone who is mentally ill, or simply lying. He goes away and ponders.

He decides to put her away (he would divorce her, because to brake an engagement in those days required the full proceedings of a divorce), but to do so privately to cause her the least pain that he can inflict by his decision. To submit would cost him dearly, and how could he believe her?

Then God speaks to him, and he knows now that submitting to God means submitting to Mary and trusting her, too. The male submits to the female in trust! For people in Joseph's day, this was front-page news! And an angelic visit to persuade him was all the more newsworthy.

The story cannot be more pointed. Submitting to God means *submitting to each other out of reverence for God.*

Submitting to God means learning (perhaps the more demanding lesson) that we *must* submit to each other if love is to have a chance. Even in good marriages where the wife accepts and believes that she must submit to the husband in all things, I have noticed a good deal of male submission going on, too. A totally one-sided submission threatens feelings of equality and promotes bitterness and low self-images. Successful marriages — no matter what

© 2020 Ray W. Lincoln

the individuals believe — are mutually submissive operations of a sort.

God helped Joseph by assuring him that Mary was telling the truth, but it was still the sight of Mary – pregnant — that his emotions had to live with each day. It was all made possible for him and his emotions by the path called trust. His trust in her *allowed* him to submit to her and her pleas without losing his own sense of equality in the relationship. Trust does that.

I know the criticism of this way of thinking. The husband submitting to the wife? Surely that's a mistake, you say, since Ephesians 5:22 says, "Wives submit to your husbands…" "It's all there as plain as day," you argue. I, too, once thought that Joseph's case was an exception to the rule. God was asking him to submit to Mary simply because the circumstances were unusual. But I think differently now that I have read *all* that Paul said. So, it came as a surprise to me to learn that we must not begin reading at verse 22 of Ephesians 5, unless we want to rip it out of context. We must begin at verse 21: ***"Submit to one another out of reverence to Christ…"*** (Emphasis mine).

Ephesians was written by the Apostle Paul in the universal language of his world, the language of Greek. In Greek, like in English, a sentence must have a verb. We know that this Greek sentence begins at verse 21 because verse

© 2020 Ray W. Lincoln

22 does not have a verb in the Greek and, grammatically, the verb for verse 22 *is in verse 21!* Why have so many Bible teachers not noticed this? Maybe partly because most of them read it in the English translations instead of in the Greek. However, Paul wrote his letter in Greek, not English! The mistakes of translators or teachers are not to be touted as the Word of God.

Here's how it translates when we pay attention to the one verb that defines where the sentence begins and ends:

"Submit to one another out of reverence to Christ, wives to your husbands, as unto the Lord."

One sentence! This is the correct translation, and as near to a literal translation of the Greek as possible. Where does the sentence start we ask again? It begins with the phrase, "Submit to one another…" That governs all the phrases that follow. Both husband and wife, we are told, must submit to each other!

In Christ there is no difference between male and female (as Paul consistently says elsewhere). Both are equal, which means the votes are equal, and God's way for fulfillment in marriage is mutual submission.

© 2020 Ray W. Lincoln

God's Way for Fulfillment in Marriage Is Mutual Submission

Then what do we make of the last part of the sentence which says "…wives to your husbands"? All we can make of it is that there must have been a particular reason (in the peculiar circumstances of Ephesus and the world of Paul's day) that explains Paul's added emphasis in verse 22 that singles out the wives. Maybe there was also a circumstance that explains the command that singles out husbands to love their wives in verse 25.

Here is the unusual circumstance as far as we can tell. At least it explains the tension in this sentence. In Paul's world, wives were treated as chattels; and husbands commonly had mistresses. To the husband, the wife was the necessary work horse for raising a family, and the mistress was his pleasure, his lover. The wife typically couldn't even go out of the house without the husband's permission. She was living in an unequal relationship and was severely oppressed. When they both became followers of Jesus, Paul had to tell the husbands to love their wives — not a mistress. And to the wife, who now over-reacted to her freedom and equality in Jesus and who didn't want to submit to her husband's wishes anymore (since he had so hurtfully abused her), Paul emphasized her need to submit to her husband. It reads as though he said, "And, you wives, don't forget you have to submit to your husbands, too." First, both must submit to each other (verse 21). And then, "You wives, you must submit to

© 2020 Ray W. Lincoln

your husbands as well" (verse 22)… and, "you husbands, love your wives, not your mistresses."

However (and I'm repeating myself for the sake of emphasis), he has already laid down the principle *that governs all things in a marriage* relationship — namely, each must submit to the other, verse 21. The votes are equal. God's way is the way of mutual submission.

So, Joseph submitted to Mary. The emotional trauma of this submission on Joseph's part that began their marriage signaled a different type of relationship from the culture of the day.

Each marriage must choose which partner is number one and settle for an unequal relationship or (much better) settle for submitting to each other, which is God's plan. Some cultures have had a difficult time of this choice, but biblical psychology and biblical exegesis demands God's way.

© 2020 Ray W. Lincoln

Leadership and Submission

Does submitting to each other mean that there are two leaders? "Two leaders" doesn't work, just like two steering wheels in a car doesn't work! No. Leadership is not a matter of having the casting vote. But in the closeness of the marriage relationship, it is receiving the nod to go ahead and lead as Christ leads his Church.

He does this in a rather interesting way. He calls for submission and then hands out free choice to his followers. He doesn't want followers who feel forced to accept his leadership. He leads by influence and moral or divine authority. No follower of Jesus has complained that he or she was forced into an oppressive relationship with their Lord. (Note your feelings: even though he is our LORD, we do not find ourselves forced by him into submission.)

Now note the parallel: Regardless of who leads (or to use the automobile metaphor, "whoever has the hands on the wheel"), the other does not feel controlled! Mutual submission, respect, and individual freedom are all called for in the closest possible bond that we have in the human family. That's how it must be to follow the way God designed it.

Leadership is not determined by who submits. Rather, it is characterized by influence and a love we find hard to give — the love of total selflessness. That's why true leadership is a challenge.

© 2020 Ray W. Lincoln

Now for the ultimate revelation about marriage relationships: who has the last say?

Well, God has, since the marriage relationship where he is honored is a three way relationship. There are three — not one — in the relationship! If all three votes are cast, one is either the casting vote or the creation of a majority vote. This is how it works. If it is a majority vote we can outvote God. That is not the plan! If God has the casting vote, he is able to have the final say in all that we do. God has the casting vote in our marriage. Prayer is, then, a prime task in following his lead.

Which way do you want your marriage to work? What you decide will determine the quality of your marriage when your votes conflict with each other or when they conflict with God's.

I don't need to point out all the benefits of God's leadership. My task is to ask that you make the right choice of leader.

© 2020 Ray W. Lincoln

Trust in God and in Each Other Provides the Structure to Withstand the Storms

Rough times lay ahead for Mary and Joseph. Can we even imagine what these two had to go through in explaining to neighbors why the baby came so early? Did Joseph confess that he had succumbed to the temptation of sex before marriage (when he actually hadn't) to protect Mary? No one else was going to believe Mary's story. Her story placed her in danger. They must have been stigmatized by the town folks, and it seems as though Joseph may have taken the blame.

A child outside of marriage was a social disaster in those days. And what of Joseph's possible loss of business? He was a carpenter, remember. Did the little community boycott his services? Perhaps (as we suggested earlier) he had to travel to the nearby Greek town that was being built some seven miles away for work and be inconvenienced, at best.

Furthermore, what did it mean for the baby when the neighbor's children called him illegitimate because he was apparently the child of a premature union. The parents' hearts must have bled for him. Jesus suffered this? Most likely and, to our wonder, it didn't turn him bitter!

© 2020 Ray W. Lincoln

When the storms break, does our trust in our partner prove unassailable? Have we learned the essentials of submission from our best teacher, God?

Love glues the relationship together and provides the attraction.
We know little about Joseph and Mary's love for each other. However, we know, if people trust and submit to each other in a common purpose, love for each other is cultivated.

© 2020 Ray W. Lincoln

Love Must Have a Foundation on Which to Grow

That foundation is the theme of this booklet: mutual submission.

Love becomes the glue of marriage and provides the attraction. Love holds relationships together through adverse times only if that love is firmly rooted. To better understand this, let's examine love more closely.

Love is built on trust. We don't love someone whom we don't trust. We may come to distrust a partner, and the next thing we notice is that our love is lost — swept away with the departure of respect.

The closer we examine the relationships of trust, respect, submission, and love, the more we have learned how dependent love is on a solid foundation of respect, trust, and submission.

Trust and respect are close cousins. Submission is the natural interaction of the forces of trust and respect in a relationship. This formula sets out the relationship.

When Paul began with "Submit to each other out of reverence for Christ," he pointed to where we get the energy for submitting to each other. The power comes from reverence, respect, honor, and trust <u>for Christ</u>.

© 2020 Ray W. Lincoln

Submission not only oils a relationship; it also fuels it. Please don't believe the lie that submission undermines self-respect. When rightly understood, it builds it. To submit is not to act as inferior.

© 2020 Ray W. Lincoln

Trials Are What Bond a Marriage

They Are the Test – the Building Inspector's Examination

Finally, it's important to remember that reading back into the marriage what we can see from the results illuminates the principles of marital success. All marriages that succeed show a deep respect that comes from submission to each other and each other's needs.

Every marriage will be tested — perhaps not as dramatically as Mary and Joseph's, but the tests will reveal what the marriage is made of, and what it is in need of most.

If you are losing your love, it's because of a lack of respect, lack of trust, and lack of the natural activity that nurtures them: submission. Go back to the basics. Submit to each other and relearn mutual respect. Submitting to each other encourages respect. Remember, respect is a result of certain conditions. Submitting reestablishes those conditions.

Submission demands something from our wills. Our wills most often stand in the way of progress in relationships. The hostile conditions to good relationships on earth are to be found in all those attitudes that elevate the idea of having to "look after number one." When we do put ourselves first we feed our selfishness. That stiffens the back of our wills and we become more self-protective. Didn't Jesus say, "Do to others as you would have them do to you?" That's a certain program for the devaluing of selfish attitudes.

So we can't expect to reestablish respect without a return to mutual submission. Mutual submission has a definition: Do to others as you would have them do to you, and be very positive about it. Create in your home the world that you would love to have as you practice mutual submission, and you will most often find it given in return.

In our society submission is not in vogue, unfortunately. Don't miss the point that submission's low image in our society is accompanied by a high rate of marriage breakdown. Homes are, for the most part, no longer incubators of respect and honor either. We must accept our part in what has happened.

The marriage of Joseph and Mary (and they wouldn't mind who's name came first) is a potent message of the need of mutual submission for a society that is struggling to keep the family unit together but losing the tussle because they have neglected the challenge.

RAY W. LINCOLN

Ray W. Lincoln is the bestselling author of I'M a KEEPER and is the founder of Ray W. Lincoln & Associates. Ray is a professional consultant and an expert in human nature. His 40 plus years of experience in speaking, teaching, and consulting began in New Zealand and have carried him to Australia and the United States. He speaks with energy and enthusiasm before large and small audiences.

It was not by accident that he became the international speaker and coach that he is today and acquired the ability to guide so many to a happier, healthier, more fulfilled life. Ray has studied extensively in the fields of Philosophy, Temperament Psychology, and Personology. A member of the National Speakers Association, his expertise has been used as a lecturer and professor, teacher and keynote speaker, seminar presenter, counselor, and coach. He teaches and leads in staff trainings, university student retreats, and parents' educational classes, as well as other seminars and training events. He also trains and mentors teachers and other professionals and executives — all with the goal of understanding each other through a biblical perspective.

www.ingramcontent.com/pod-product-compliance
Lightning Source LLC
Chambersburg PA
CBHW071751020426
42331CB00008B/2267